BRITAIN IN OLD PHOTOGRAPHS

KENT

CHRISTINE DUNN

Budding BOOKS

A Budding Book

First published in 1996 by Sutton Publishing Limited

This edition first published in 1998 by Budding Books, an imprint of
Sutton Publishing Limited · Phoenix Mill · Thrupp · Stroud · Gloucestershire GL5 2BU

Jacket photographs: *front*: Holiday-makers on the sands at Broadstairs, 1907; *back*: Motorcycle taxi in the West Malling area. Pictured are Ray Barton and his wife Mary. Ray was the youngest son of Freda Barton, the photographer. Freda was a commercial photographer working in West Malling from about 1905 to 1940; *title page*: Visitors step aboard to inspect the L53 at Chatham Naval Dockyard, *c.* 1935.

A catalogue record for this book is available from the British Library.

ISBN 1 84015 088 2

Typeset in 10/12 Perpetua.
Typesetting and origination by
Sutton Publishing Limited.
Printed in Great Britain by
WBC Limited, Bridgend, Mid-Glamorgan.

Children outside the Grand Picture Palace, Holborough Road, Snodland, after a Saturday afternoon performance, *c.* 1930.

CONTENTS

The Chequers Inn, High Street, Tonbridge, *c.* 1900. The inn was reputedly featured in some of Jeffrey Farnol's novels.

INTRODUCTION

Kent, so often referred to as 'The Garden of England', is much more than a county of hops and oasthouses, apple and cherry orchards, stately homes and beautiful parkland, beaches and candy floss. Most people who live in Kent reside in its towns, not its much photographed villages. This book is devoted to those towns and cities, large and small.

Some places such as Canterbury or Dover are famed throughout the land whereas others are mainly known to those who live in the county. What is apparent from looking at the photographs gathered together for this volume is the diversity of Kent towns. The contrast between the small market town and great cathedral city, or the town with a manufacturing base and the brash seaside resort could not be more marked.

Kent over the centuries has benefited and suffered from its unique geographical position within the United Kingdom. Being the closest area to continental Europe it has been at the forefront of most invasions or would-be invasions, from Julius Caesar to the Second World War. It also has been the embarkation and disembarkation point for those leaving or returning to England, whether they left in peace or war. Today Kent is still under constant development as the gateway to Europe. The Channel Tunnel and high-speed railway mean more road and rail links and increasing urbanisation.

Many of the pictures in this book were taken at the end of the nineteenth or in the early part of this century. Some places are still instantly recognisable but others have changed greatly. Most Kent towns were established centuries before the coming of the motor car and it is modern-day traffic that has caused huge changes, with roads being built or widened, buildings demolished and the pattern of shopping moved from town centres to large out-of-town retail outlets.

There are some themes which recur in the photographs, such as the presence of the military and the many surviving fortifications, the problems of flooding and storm damage and the very strong maritime connections, which perhaps best illustrate the topography and history of this fascinating part of England.

As you browse through this book I hope you will find images that appeal or that bring back memories or perhaps encourage you to discover the local history of your own town or village. Most of the photographs included in this publication are from the Local

Studies Collections maintained in the town centre libraries and the collection kept at the Centre for Kentish Studies in Maidstone. Over many years Kent Libraries have collected illustrations on their locality, resulting in a unique pictorial record. The Arts and Libraries Department welcomes further donations, or the loan of photographs that can be copied.

I am indebted to my library colleagues for their assistance. Although the final choice of illustrations is mine, I could not have produced this book without the initial selections they made from the collections in their libraries and for the time, effort and expertise they put into providing information for the captions.

Christine Dunn
Local Studies Liaison Officer
Arts and Libraries
Kent County Council

Royal Marines from Deal on an outing in Kent, 1913.

SECTION ONE

FROM THE THAMES TO THE GREENSAND RIDGE

Dartford, Gravesend, Swanley, Westerham, Sevenoaks, West Malling

Floods at Dartford, 1910. There were many towns in Kent which suffered serious flooding over the centuries. This scene is outside the post office in Lowfield Street.

General view of Dartford from the Upper Burial Ground, East Hill, *c.* 1910. This was one of the main routes into the town and gives a view of shops, houses, industries and Holy Trinity Church.

The town bridge over the River Darent, Dartford, *c.* 1910. The row of shops on the right was known locally as The Chicken Run.

Dartford High Street, *c.* 1900. The local traders set up stalls outside their shops for the Saturday market. The Norman tower of Holy Trinity Church is seen in the background.

Dartford High Street, 1961. Many of the old public houses and shops still flourished at this time.

Frozen millpond, Dartford, 1895. The firm of Burroughs Wellcome and Co. has been in the town since 1889 and their factory was adapted from the Phoenix Paper Mill building.

Dartford Creek, early 1950s. Paper-making was an important local industry and here wood pulp and esparto grass are being unloaded for the mills.

Women workers at Dartford during the First World War. J. & E. Hall, the engineering firm, was famous throughout the world for its manufactures. During the First World War more than 300 women were recruited to fill the gap left by the men. They became, for example, skilled crane drivers and welders and their contribution was incalculable, as the firm was producing war material by then.

Entrance to Dartford Brewery Company, 1910. There was a brewery on this site in Lowfield Street from the late seventeenth century until 1925. The photograph was taken on General Election day. The men are, from left to right, Percival Gibbard, Gilbert Tatner, Frederick Thomsett, Harvey Hogg and Leonard Gibbard. The horses were named Boxer, Gypsy and Sanger.

Daren flour mills, Dartford, *c.* 1910. This was one of several mills in the area and was situated on the banks of Dartford Creek. In 1929 the firm became Daren Ltd, famous for its brown bread and biscuits.

Gravesend from the River Thames, 1831. This view of the town shows the Landing Place at the bottom of the High Street, used by watermen for landing passengers until the building of the town pier in 1834.

Rosherville Gardens, Northfleet, 1868. These gardens were popular with day trippers from London. The Italian Gardens pictured here were one of the attractions, which included a bear pit, aviary, monkey cages, a maze, a theatre and banqueting hall. At the height of its popularity there were over 15,000 visitors a day. The gardens closed in 1900.

Opening of the clock tower, Gravesend, 1889. Built to mark Queen Victoria's Golden Jubilee this local landmark is over 50 ft high and took two years to complete.

Milton Road, Gravesend, *c.* 1910. The clock tower is very much in evidence with St John's Roman Catholic Church on the left.

King Street, Gravesend, 1903. An open-top tram on its way to Northfleet is passing the Gravesend and Milton National Schools near the junction with Windmill Street.

Top of Gravesend High Street, 1910: the junction of the High Street with New Road and King Street, showing Bryant and Rackstraw's drapery and haberdashery store and the New Prince of Orange Hotel.

Town Pier, Gravesend, mid-1920s. The pier was built in 1834 to replace the previous landing stage. This view shows the entrance to the pier when it was the Gravesend station for the London, Tilbury and Southend section of the London, Midland and Scottish Railway Company.

The Promenade, Gravesend, *c.* 1900. The Gordon Promenade was constructed in the 1880s on a stretch of tidal shoreway, to create an area above the level of the river. It was built using cement bags, purchased after they were damaged when the schooner carrying them sank. The view also shows the Royal Terrace Pier.

The Great Frost of 1895. This view of Gravesend's riverfront shows the ice-bound bawley boats and the large ice boulders into which the River Thames had turned during this very hard winter.

Regatta Day, Gravesend, *c.* 1890. A typical view of the promenade and the River Thames, showing the large numbers of spectators the regatta attracted at this time.

Aerial view of Swanley, *c.* 1930. The picture shows in the left foreground St Mary's Church, and prominently placed are the Alexandra Hospital and Whiteoak Hospital; the Asda store is now on this site.

Azalea Avenue and Greenacres Estate, Swanley, early 1960s. A great deal of construction work was taking place at this time.

Staff at Whiteoak Hospital, Swanley. Probably photographed early in the twentieth century, Whiteoak Hospital was one of several hospitals in Swanley at this time. It was a hospital treating children with eye diseases.

The smoking room, St Bart's Hospital, Convalescent Home, Swanley. St Bart's Hospital, or Kettlewell as it was also known, was opened in 1885. The Alexandra Hospital moved to the site in 1920.

Cattle market, Westerham, 1860. This very old photograph shows the weekly market. It was held in the Market Square and High Street.

Market Square, Westerham, 1926. Some of the buildings shown in the previous picture are clearly visible more than sixty years later. This view, with the horse trough and drinking fountain which were previously on The Green, is looking down to the High Street and The Green.

The Green, Westerham, 1830s. This scene is dominated by the old Buttery which the artist has exaggerated in size. It was removed at the end of the nineteenth century and a smaller one built in its place.

The Green, Westerham, 1926. Photographed nearly a century after the previous picture, the scene still has some familiar landmarks. The memorial to General James Wolfe, unveiled in 1911 to commemorate Westerham's famous son, is the focal point. The First World War Memorial Gun was removed and melted down during the Second World War to help the war effort.

Sir Winston Churchill at Chartwell, near Westerham. Chartwell was Churchill's home from 1924 until the end of his life. This photograph shows him building a wall. In 1928 he caused controversy in trade union circles by taking out a card as an adult apprentice in the Amalgamated Union of Building Trade Workers. A bronze statue to him now stands on The Green at Westerham.

Westerham railway station, *c.* 1910. This shows not only the staff assembled on the platform, but also milk churns, a sack barrow and adverts for various products. The station operated for eighty years, closing on 28 October 1961.

Junction of the High Street and London Road, Sevenoaks. A cattle market was held here and in the late nineteenth century a fountain was added in front of Mr Corke's shop.

London Road, Sevenoaks, 1900. In winter Kent can experience severe weather conditions, as can be seen in this view.

Royal Oak Hotel, Upper High Street, Sevenoaks, 1880s. This was one of the main coaching inns in the area. The stagecoach is a genuine coach, purchased by the proprietor of the hotel; this photograph captured its last journey.

Traffic chaos at Riverhead, near Sevenoaks, 1960s. Sevenoaks and the surrounding area was well known for its traffic jams before the opening of motorways and bypasses. The garage and other buildings in this view were later demolished to widen the road.

Smith's Brewery, Sevenoaks, *c.* 1900. This brewery, which stood in the High Street, was one of the few industries in Sevenoaks at the time. Brewing was to be found in many Kentish towns at the beginning of the century.

Granada Cinema, Sevenoaks, 1951. This cinema was built on the site of Smith's Brewery and is shown here decorated for the Festival of Britain. It closed in 1960 and was eventually demolished. The site is where Suffolk Way joins the High Street.

Station Parade, Sevenoaks. This picture was probably taken in the late 1920s or early 1930s. Sevenoaks (Tubs Hill) station is on the left and the shops on the right are still retail outlets today.

Rail disaster at Sevenoaks (Tubs Hill) railway station, 7 June 1884. This collision of two goods trains resulted in the loss of two lives and considerable destruction of rolling stock and platforms.

Sevenoaks Town Band, 1903. The members of the band are pictured on the Vine. The band was formed in 1890 and is still in existence today.

Sevenoaks Home Guard, during the Second World War. In a scene reminiscent of the TV series *Dad's Army* members of the 20th (Sevenoaks) Battalion Kent Home Guard are undertaking exercises for camouflage purposes.

Vine Cricket Ground, Sevenoaks, *c.* 1900. This photograph shows the famous Vine Cricket Ground before the demolition of these old houses. Kent has a long tradition of cricket being played in the county. The earliest published record of cricket at Sevenoaks is of a match held on 6 September 1734.

Sevenoaks Cricket Bi-Centenary Week, July 1934. This was organised to commemorate two hundred years of cricket being played at Sevenoaks. This shows a rehearsal at Sevenoaks School's cricket ground of the match to be played on 21 July, replicating a cricket match of two hundred years ago.

High Street, West Malling, 1886.

Swan Hotel, West Malling, *c.* 1925. The Swan had been a coaching inn with livery stables to the rear of the building. The proprietors, when this photograph was taken, were Mr and Mrs Bex who are pictured in the doorway on the right. The manager, Mr Baker, is shown on the left. The false painted timbered front was added by Mr and Mrs Bex and has since been removed.

Shops in the High Street, West Malling. In the foreground is a steam lorry owned by George Hide, which was a well-known sight on the local village streets of the area.

Military funeral procession, West Malling, 1915. The funeral was for a Canadian soldier, Private W.R. Dobson, who was killed in a traffic accident. The procession is passing Malling House, where the soldier had been convalescing.

SECTION TWO

ALONG THE MEDWAY

Gillingham, Chatham, Rochester, Strood, Snodland, Maidstone, Tonbridge

Medway Mission to Seamen, 1932. Mr J. Neilson is distributing parcels to those who will be spending Christmas at sea.

High Street, Gillingham, 1960s. Small businesses are very much in evidence. On the left is a small Marks and Spencer store, which had opened in 1912 as a penny bazaar and which closed in 1990.

A summer day at Gillingham Strand, 1950s. The swimming pool to the left was opened in 1896. During the 1940s the Strand developed as a pleasure ground when many residents had to stay at home for their holidays.

Jezreels Tower, Gillingham. This tower was a landmark in Gillingham for over seventy years. It was built by James Jershom Jezreel and his followers, in the belief that the millennium would mark the coming of Christ's Kingdom on Earth for the next thousand years. The tower remained unfinished but it was not demolished until 1961.

Unveiling of the statue to General Gordon of Khartoum, 19 May 1890. The memorial was unveiled by the Prince of Wales (later Edward VII) at the Royal Engineers' Brompton Barracks, Gillingham.

James McCudden VC. McCudden, a top fighter pilot of the First World War, was born in Gillingham and lived at Belmont Road. He is pictured in 1918 standing in front of his favourite bi-plane. He was killed in July 1918 when his plane crashed in France.

'Fireman's Wedding' tragedy, Gillingham, 1929. This was part of the funeral procession following the tragedy at Gillingham Park fête on 11 July 1929 when fifteen people, including nine boys, lost their lives. A fire started prematurely when the fire brigade was undertaking a demonstration to rescue a wedding party from a replica house.

Gillingham Wharf, *c.* 1930. This area is now known as Gillingham Pier. The boys are playing with home-made 'barrows', which were constructed from orange boxes and pram wheels.

Sailors coming ashore at Gillingham Pier. This was probably Christmas 1941 and they were from HMS *Renown* anchored off Sheerness. They were brought by small boats or lighters to Gillingham Pier.

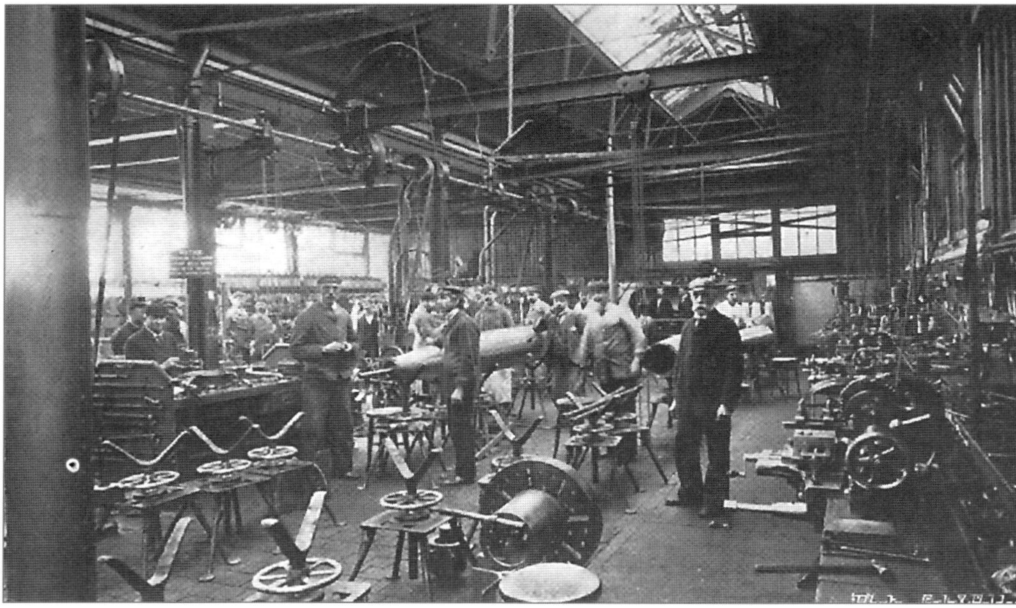

Torpedo fitting room, Chatham Dockyard, *c.* 1910. Although the dockyard is named Chatham Dockyard it is situated in both Chatham and Gillingham. Until its closure, it saw four centuries of service to the Royal Navy. It is now a living museum.

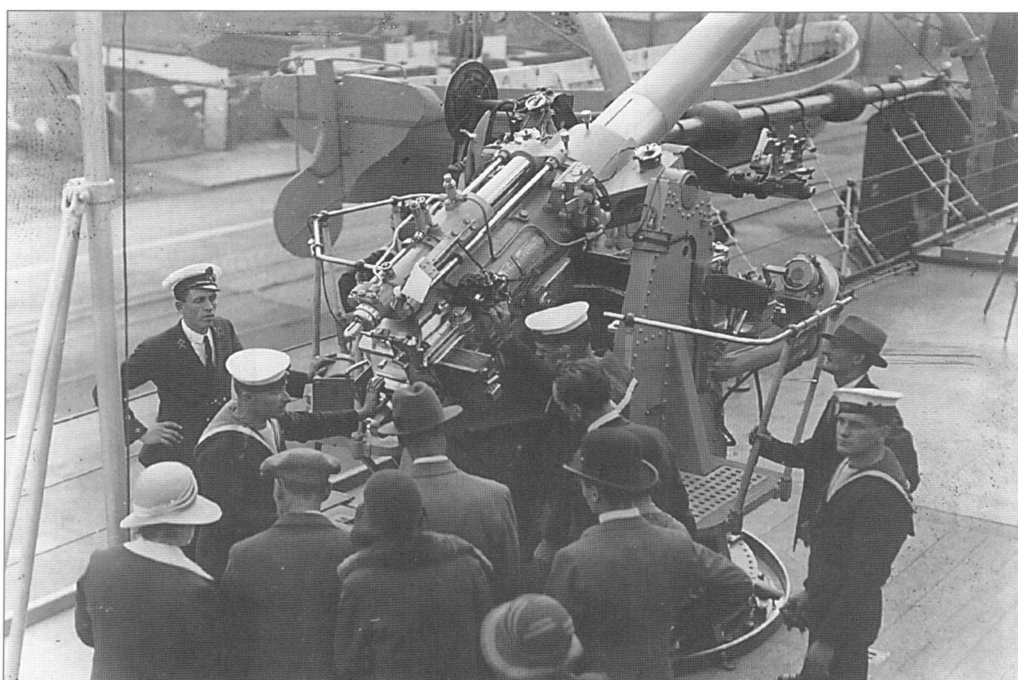

Chatham Navy Week, 1932. These open days were held annually and were very popular. Here visitors inspect an anti-aircraft gun.

Chatham from the air, 1949. A panorama of the town showing the River Medway with Sun Pier and St Mary's Church. The Town Hall is in the centre of the picture and the town centre before redevelopment may be picked out.

Chatham Town Hall Gardens, *c.* 1910. The old cemetery was laid out as a public park and it afforded fine views of the town and river.

Chatham from the Medway, *c.* 1900. This shows the Marine Barracks and St Mary's Church in the distance. The church was being rebuilt at the time. It now houses the Medway Heritage Centre.

Chatham High Street East, *c.* 1905. The present day High Street has been altered beyond all recognition from this early view.

Rochester from the Medway, 1890. The Norman castle's strategic position is clearly shown, and the cathedral, in the centre of the picture, is seen before remodelling of the tower. A Thames barge has lowered its mast and sails ready to pass under Rochester Bridge.

Rochester Castle, 1891. The gardens were later cleared to make an open space for the 1931 pageant.

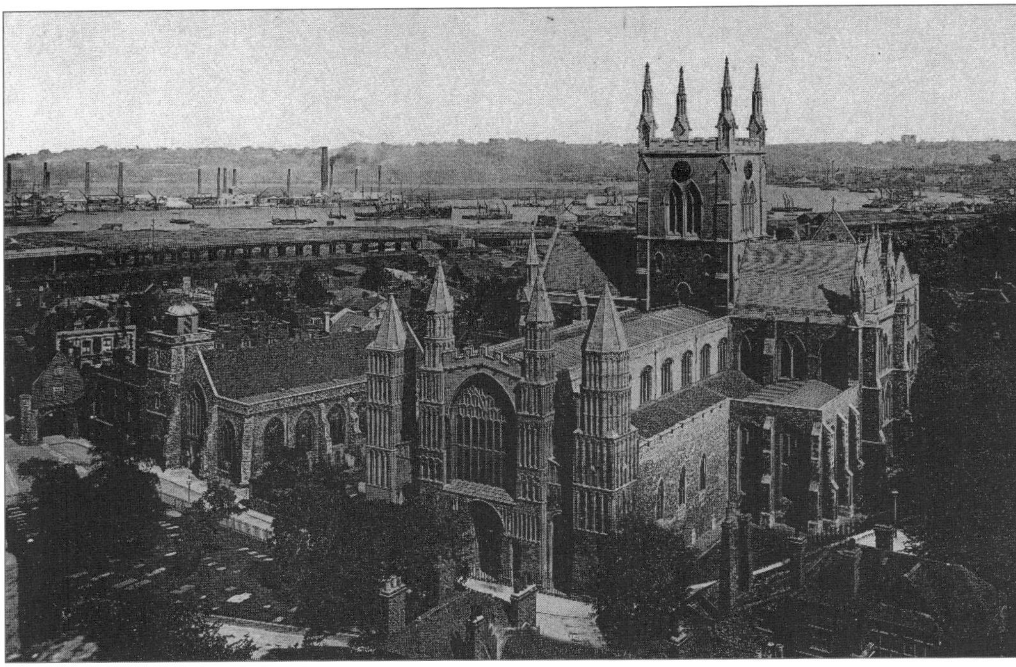

Rochester and the Medway from the castle, 1897. The cathedral is the focal point of this panorama showing both the houses in Boley Hill, adjacent to the cathedral, and the busy river in the distance.

Rochester High Street, June 1911. The coronation of George V was celebrated Empire-wide, and Rochester High Street was not to be outdone with its display of flags and bunting.

Poor Travellers' House, High Street, Rochester, 1909. The benefactor, Richard Watts, endowed the charity which administers this house. Until 1940 free bed and board was offered each night to no more than six travellers who could not afford lodging elsewhere.

Poor Travellers' House, Rochester, *c.* 1920. Four hopefuls knock at the solid front door in search of a night's free accommodation. Charles Dickens ensured the fame of the house with his tale *Seven Poor Travellers*.

New Road, Rochester, *c.* 1915. A tram passes St Bartholomew's Hospital en route for Brompton. This pleasant tree-lined boulevard was later widened and, sadly, the trees were felled.

The *Medway Queen* paddlesteamer, another form of transport familiar to local people during the first half of the century. The *Medway Queen* was built in 1924 and remained in service until 1963. She is now undergoing restoration.

The Admiralty Court in annual session on a barge at Rochester, 1937. The Medway fisheries gave employment to dredgermen working the oysterbeds in the past. The demise of the industry means only a very few fishermen remain.

Rochester Bridge, 1914. There has been a crossing at approximately this point since Roman times and it has been a vital element in the growth and strategic importance of Rochester. The rail bridge is seen behind the road bridge.

Strood Docks, 1930. The Thames and Medway Canal Tunnel can be seen in the distance. The canal opened in 1824 but the arrival of the railway ensured its rapid decline. It closed as a through route to shipping in 1845.

Strood Hill, London Road, 1900. This road is still a vital artery through and to the Medway towns. In 1900 it was the main approach route from London.

Angel Corner, Strood. Tolls were collected at the turnpike gate at Angel Corner until 1876.

Strood High Street, *c.* 1930. The Invicta Cinema opened in 1919 and operated until bomb damage forced its temporary closure in 1945. After the war it reopened as the Wardona but only lasted until 1959. A small supermarket is now on the site.

Strood and Frindsbury Voluntary Aid Detachment (VAD) Hospital, First World War. Staff and volunteers pose with patients outside Cypress House, which was used as an annexe to the hospital. Many towns and villages in Kent had VAD hospitals.

Bread and Cheese Hill, Strood, 25 April 1906. This shows those who participated in the annual custom of 'beating the bounds' of the parish; at this date it would appear that most thought it an unsuitable activity for the ladies!

Church Field, Snodland, 1908. Snodland grew as an industrial village in the late nineteenth and early twentieth centuries. Its proximity to the River Medway helped industry to expand. This view shows the Townsend Hook Paper Mill in the background.

Fire at the Townsend Hook Paper Mill, Snodland, 12 August 1906.

Brook Street School, Snodland, *c.* 1905. An interior view showing the layout of the schoolroom; the headmaster is on the left. Note the line of rifles, probably kept there because it was not unusual for local rifle volunteer corps to practise drilling in school rooms.

Staff at Brook Street School, Snodland, 1880. The headmaster, Tom Hilder, is seated in the middle and behind him is William Gooding, assistant master.

River Medway and Bridge, Maidstone. This Victorian view shows a tranquil scene looking towards the old Town Bridge.

Maidstone and the Medway, late 1960s. Many of these buildings have now gone, although the high-level bridge remains a landmark with the Tilling-Stevens building.

Week Street, Maidstone, 1936. The West Kent Hotel on the corner of Station Road closed in 1970.

Week Street, Maidstone, *c.* 1967. Taken slightly further down from the previous picture, it shows a scene more easily recognisable today. Dunnings department store is on the right, at the corner of St Faith Street, now the site of the Army and Navy Stores.

High Street, Maidstone, 1900. Maidstone was another town which suffered from the flooding of the River Medway. An interesting variety of horse-drawn vehicles is evident.

High Street, Maidstone, 1960s. This is looking towards the river in the opposite direction to the previous view. The cannon in the foreground is a Russian gun from the Crimean War, presented to the town in 1858. It is still there today.

Lower Stone Street, Maidstone, *c.* 1903. This busy scene was photographed in an area which has changed beyond recognition today.

Bomb damage in Mill Street, Maidstone. A flying bomb hit the area on 31 October 1940. A total of 70 people were killed and 124 seriously injured by bombs that fell on the town during the war.

Honnor's, 108 Week Street, Maidstone, 1890s. Alfred Honnor and staff are outside the shop which started the family business. Alfred Honnor took over the tenancy of this shop in 1890 and the corn and seed merchant's business successfully traded in Maidstone for a hundred years.

Maidstone Zoo Park, 1950s. Situated at Cobtree Manor, it was owned by Sir Garrard Tyrwhitt-Drake.

Tonbridge Castle, 1960s. Tonbridge grew up around its great medieval castle. In more recent years the lawn has been the venue for many official, social and cultural events.

The Great Bridge over the Medway, Tonbridge, early 1950s. The National Provincial Bank had occupied the site by the river since about 1919 and a bank is still there today.

Flooding at Tonbridge, October 1880. Over the years Tonbridge was regularly flooded. The water couldn't stop these cabs in the High Street, below the Little Bridge.

High Street, Tonbridge. This is the south end of the street before the road was widened in 1894. The Temperance Hotel, G. Terry's and J. Lambert's shops, on the left, were demolished to build the Free Library and Technical Institute. The Angel Hotel (right) was demolished in 1972.

Procession of children in the High Street, Tonbridge, celebrating the coronation of George V, 1911. Each child was presented with a coronation medal to wear for the event. After an adult procession, a service was held on the castle lawn.

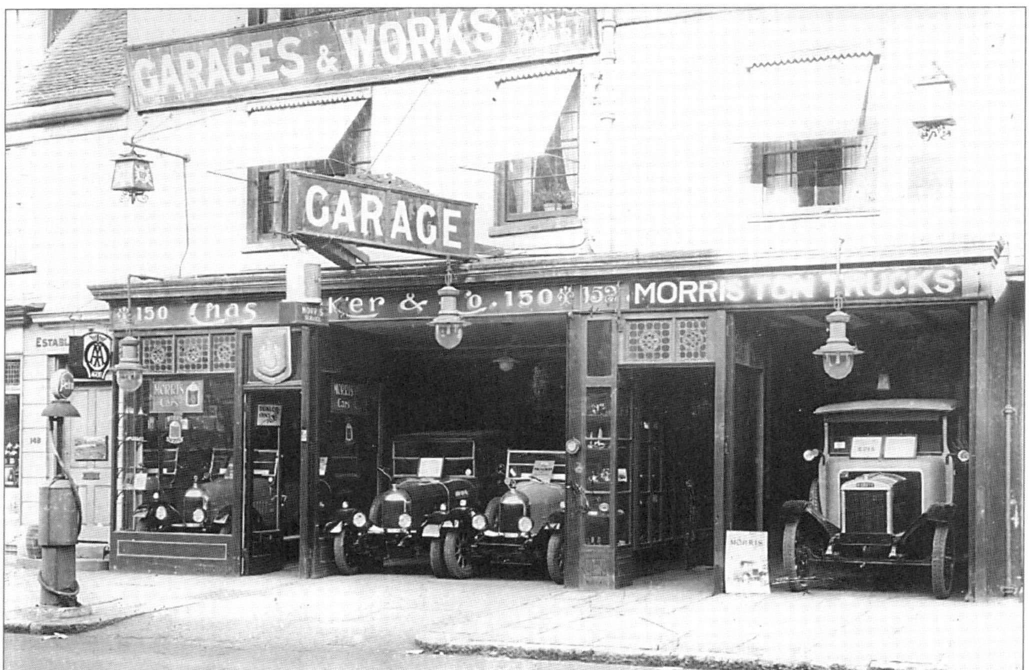

150–2 High Street, Tonbridge, 1920s. This was the premises of Chas Baker and Co., and shows the garage and what is reputed to be the first petrol pump in Tonbridge.

Norton's Boat Yard, Barden Road, Tonbridge, early 1900s. Albert Norton is pictured with his wife and family.

Tonbridge Volunteer Fire Brigade at the station behind the Rose and Crown, *c*. 1900.

Pupils and masters at one of the school houses, Tonbridge School, 1905. The public school was founded in 1553 as the Grammar School.

First World War recruits, Tonbridge, 1914. This picture was possibly taken in August 1914 and the recruits are pictured at the Royal West Kent Drill Hall (formerly the Corn Exchange) in Tonbridge Market.

SECTION THREE

THE WEALD & THE MARSH

Edenbridge, Tunbridge Wells, Cranbrook, Tenterden, New Romney, Lydd

Recreation Ground, Tenterden, 9 May 1908. Farmers are demonstrating against the importation of foreign hops.

Edenbridge parish church, 1905. This view remains much the same today, except for the lych-gate which now stands at the entrance to the churchyard.

High Street, Edenbridge, *c.* 1950. The three lime trees on the right were all that remained of an avenue planted at the turn of the century. They, in turn, were cut down in the 1960s.

High Street, Edenbridge, looking south, 1905. The inn sign for the Crown Hotel positioned across the street was a feature then as it is now.

High Street, Edenbridge, from a similar viewpoint to the previous picture, 1950s. The sweet shop and the 'library', on the left, was formerly the Half Moon beer house.

Bath Square, The Pantiles, Tunbridge Wells, 1870. The chalybeate spring was discovered by Dudley, Lord North in 1606, while returning to London from Lord Abergavenny's residence in Eridge. The bath house shown in this picture was erected behind the spring in about 1805.

Visitors 'taking the waters' at Tunbridge Wells, *c.* 1900. In the foreground can be seen the 'dipper' who was responsible for dispensing the spring water from the stone basin.

A band playing on The Pantiles, Tunbridge Wells, *c.* 1875. A band could be found playing on The Parade every morning at eleven o'clock.

The Fishmarket, The Pantiles, *c.* 1870. Although early plans of the area show a fishmarket as far back as 1725, this building wasn't erected until the late eighteenth century. Tolson's ran the market from the 1840s to the 1920s.

Mount Edgecombe, The Common, Tunbridge Wells, *c.* 1890. In the middle-left of the picture can be seen the Lower Cricket Ground.

High Street, Tunbridge Wells, *c.* 1905. On the left is the premises of Goulden and Curry, stationers and subscription library, founded before 1840. It became a well-known bookshop in 1908, finally closing in 1986.

Lower end of Mount Pleasant, Tunbridge Wells, *c.* 1900–6. Central station is on the left, showing the original clock tower.

Central station, Tunbridge Wells, 1880. This was built on the site of Bell's Brewery in 1846. In 1912 the 'down' side of the station was completely rebuilt with a new clock tower.

Royal Victoria and Sussex Hotel, The Pantiles, *c.* 1870. The hotel closed soon after this photograph was taken, in 1880. On the ground floor were the Lower Assembly Rooms. The rooms were used for dancing, gambling and tea-drinking.

Spa Hotel, Tunbridge Wells, 1951. Originally the home of Major Yorke of the East India Company and built in 1765, it was converted to The Spa Hydropathic Sanatorium in the 1870s. After only two years it closed and became a hotel in 1880.

Union Mill, Cranbrook, 1906. This large smock windmill which dominates Cranbrook was built in 1814 by James Humphrey, a local wheelwright. The mill is still operating today.

Stone Street, Cranbrook, *c.* 1905. The windmill is much in evidence and the weatherboarded buildings are still a feature of the town today.

Stone Street, Cranbrook, 1913. The George Hotel was where Queen Elizabeth I was received in 1573 during her visit to Cranbrook.

High Street, Cranbrook, 1960s: a busy scene in this small Wealden town, which originally owed its prosperity to the medieval cloth trade.

Town Hall, Tenterden. This photograph was taken before 1912 when a balcony was added to the building. The Woolpack Hotel next door gives an indication of the once-thriving wool trade associated with the town.

High Street, Tenterden, 22 June 1911. The people of Tenterden celebrate the coronation of George V; the procession is making its way past the Eight Bells towards West Cross.

The Toll Gate, Tenterden. The gate was removed in 1880. This view of the corner of Church Road and opposite The Pebbles shows some of the many bow-fronted shops and houses in the town which has been, over the centuries, the centre of trade for this rural part of Kent.

High Street, Tenterden, *c*. 1890. The wide tree-lined main street has a water pump in the foreground with the parish church of St Mildred behind.

Christmas time at Hook's the butchers, High Street, Tenterden, 1902.

Mercer's Shop, High Street, Tenterden. John Mercer is on the left with Charles Mercer (right) and they are proudly displaying a 17 lb cabbage. The shop moved from Station Road to the High Street in 1913. Note also the signs in the window for a bath chair for hire and cycles stored for 1*d* each.

High Street, New Romney, *c.* 1910. The New Inn on the right, despite its Georgian façade, is thought to date back to the fifteenth century, and has a number of passages said to have been used by smugglers.

New Romney, *c.* 1900. A peaceful view of the Ashford Road near where it crosses the High Street. This small town on Romney Marsh was one of the important Cinque Ports in medieval times.

The Romney, Hythe and Dymchurch Light Railway at Dungeness. Often described as the world's smallest public railway, this 15 in. gauge railway serves the towns of New Romney and Hythe and was extended to Dungeness in 1929.

Jack Ford photographed at Lydd, *c.* 1925. He was known as Jack of Dungeness and sold fish on the marsh. He is pictured outside Grisbrook Farm Cottage, Manor Road; the cottage is now the only one in Lydd with a thatched roof.

Coronation Square, Lydd, *c.* 1905. This scene shows Hutchings' General Store with the staff and inhabitants posing for the photographer. There is still a general store on the site today.

All Saints' Church, Lydd, *c.* 1898. This fine church is known as the 'Cathedral of the Marsh' and has the longest nave of any church in Kent. It was badly damaged by bombing during the Second World War but has since been restored.

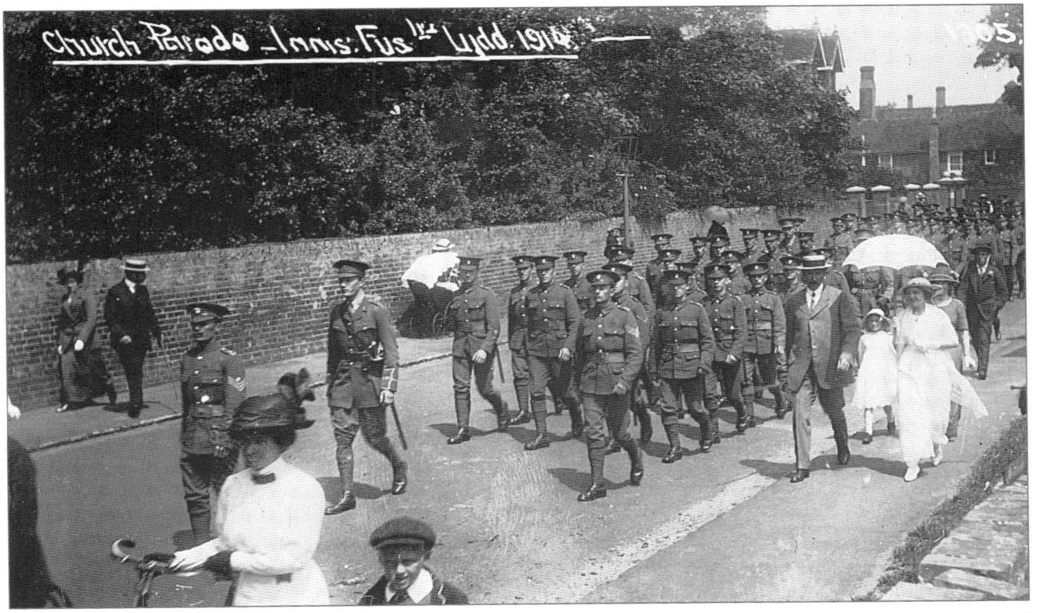

Church Parade, Lydd, 1910. The nearby Lydd Army Camp has led to the town being closely associated with the army. Here the Inniskillen Fusiliers are on parade together with local people.

Lydd, 1910. The townsfolk are seen here on the Rype after Church Parade. The school building can be seen in the centre of the view.

Lydd army camp, *c.* 1906. A battery is in action on Lydd Ranges.

Romney Marsh, *c.* 1910. The Romney breed of sheep is famous throughout the world, having been exported widely, and here can be seen an early mechanised form of sheep shearing.

SECTION FOUR

THE ENGLISH CHANNEL – PORTS & RESORTS

Hythe, Folkestone, Dover, Deal, Walmer

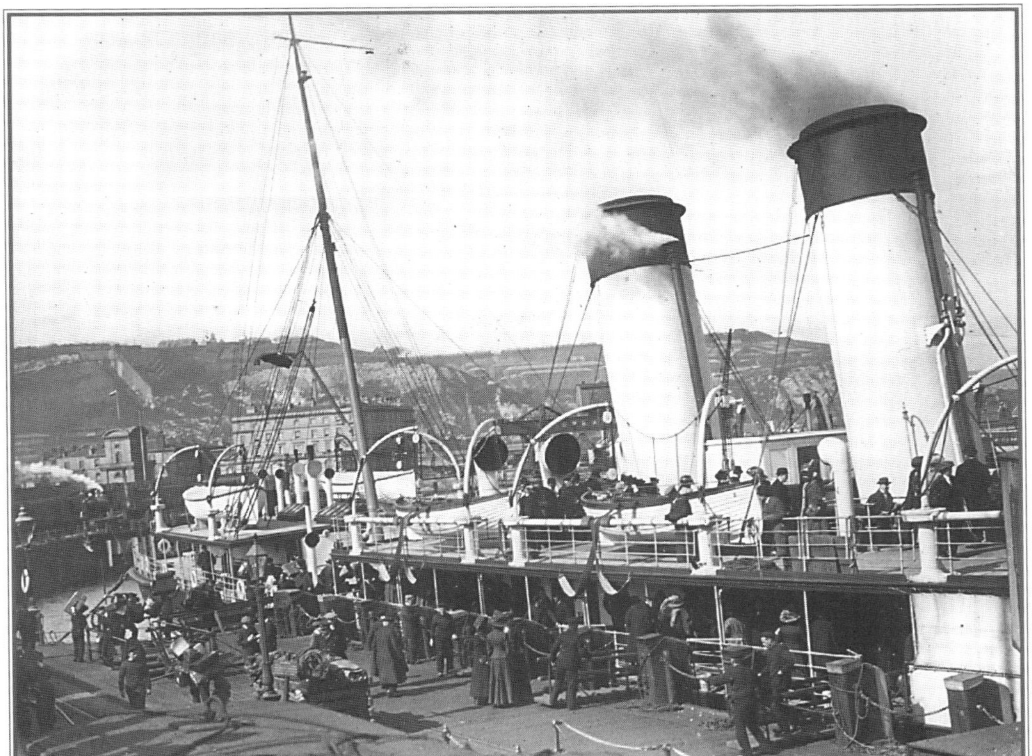

Ferry at Dover harbour, 1910. Passengers are seen here embarking for the journey to Calais.

Hythe, 1890: a view across the town to the coast, with the Imperial Hotel and Beaconsfield Terrace beyond the church.

West Parade, Hythe, 1898. The shingle beach is occupied by bathing tents and people enjoying the sea air, but they are well clad to avoid getting a sun tan, which was not acceptable at this time.

High Street, Hythe, 1898. This is one of the longest trading streets in Kent. On the right is Lovick's, a newsagent and subscription library which occupied the site from 1888 to 1936.

High Street, Hythe, 1921. The distinctive Town Hall with its clock and the bank, formerly the London and County Bank, are still unchanged today.

Royal Military Canal, Hythe, *c.* 1918. Hythe was one of the original Cinque Ports, which in medieval times, before England had a navy, were pressed into service as defenders of the realm. In later years during the threat of Napoleonic invasion this canal was cut with gun emplacements, to assist in defending this vulnerable area.

School of Musketry, Hythe, 1903. The building was begun in 1807 with accommodation for 300 men. It continued here, with a change of name to the Small Arms School, until 1968. The site is now occupied by the regional headquarters of the local electricity company.

Freedom of the Borough ceremony, Hythe, 1953. The Small Arms School Corps is returning to barracks after receiving the Freedom of the Borough. The school was also celebrating its centenary.

The Hythe and Sandgate tram, known as 'The Toast-rack', in its summer guise, *c.* 1901. The tram ran from the bottom of Sandgate Hill to Hythe and was, during the First World War, drawn by mules.

Folkestone, *c.* 1840. This print shows the harbour and The Stade with the parish church above. The scene changed rapidly when the harbour was purchased by the South Eastern Railway Company in 1843 and the railway from London brought additional prosperity to the town.

Railway viaduct, Folkestone, 1844. The brick-built viaduct, here crossing the Foord Valley, is still a major landmark today.

Sandgate Road, Folkestone. This picture was taken shortly after the Town Hall (centre) was completed in 1861 on the site of the old Cistern House.

Millfield Mill, Folkestone, 1880. This mill, built in about 1820, was removed to Bethersden in 1885. The area today is still known as Millfield.

Folkestone harbour, 1895. This view shows the inner harbour and The Bayle with the London and Paris Hotel in the centre.

Fishermen at Folkestone harbour with St Peter's Church above.

Tan-Lade (net house), The Stade, Folkestone, 1912. The railway arch for the harbour branch is visible at the end of the street.

Folkestone from the pier, *c.* 1900. The variety of entertainments available to holiday-makers is evident, such as the Bathing Establishment and Camera Obscura. The Leas Cliff lift is all that remains today.

The Leas, Folkestone, 1912. Lord Radnor owned much of Folkestone and developed it as a resort for the middle and upper classes. This scene gives an impression of what it was like in its heyday; the bandstand was erected in 1895.

High Street, Folkestone, 1890. Now renamed the Olde High Street, the street is still cobbled.

Palace Theatre, Cheriton, Folkestone. Opened as the Electric Hall in 1911, it stood on the corner of Cheriton High Street and what is now Chilham Road. It was popular with the soldiers from nearby Shorncliffe Camp but closed in 1923.

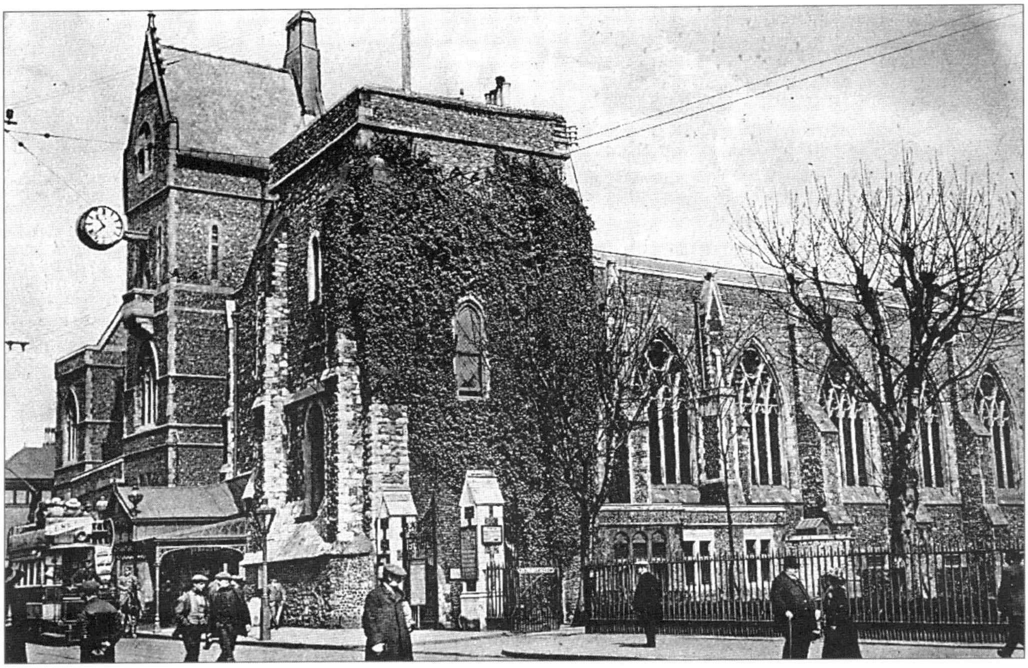

Maison Dieu, Dover, *c.* 1910. This was founded as a hospital by Hubert de Burgh in 1203, and had various uses before becoming Dover's Town Hall. The Connaught Hall on the left was added in 1883.

The Court of Brotherhood and Guestling, Dover 1902. This photograph was taken on the steps of the Maison Dieu in the year of Edward VII's coronation. As a baron of the Cinque Ports Henry Martyn Mowll, Mayor of Dover, had the privilege of attending the coronation.

Custom House Quay, overlooking Granville Dock, Dover, *c.* 1900. The famous Ship Hotel where Queen Victoria stayed as a child is seen in the centre, and on the Western Heights above are the Grand Shaft Barracks.

Wellington Dock, Dover, *c.* 1905. In the distance the Admiralty Pier is in the process of being extended. The Prince of Wales Pier on the left had been completed in 1902. Dover remains today the only one of the Cinque Ports still to have a thriving port.

Dover beach, 1890. Holiday-makers are relaxing on the beach with the famous white cliffs and Dover Castle behind.

Promenade Pier, Dover, *c.* 1905. The pier was built in 1893 with a pavilion added in 1901 to provide entertainment. It suffered damage and financial difficulties and was acquired by the Admiralty before the First World War, never to be used again as a pleasure pier. It was demolished in 1927.

Carnival procession in Woolcomber Street, Dover, 1930s. On the left is the distinctive wrought-iron public convenience. Unfortunately, none of the buildings survived the Second World War.

Biggin Street, Dover, *c.* 1909. This is one of Dover's main shopping streets. St Mary's Church is in the centre of the view.

Market Square, Dover, *c.* 1905. A busy market day with a tram on the right.

St James Street, Dover, 1920s. Dover Castle dominates this street scene in which, owing to bomb damage during the Second World War, every building visible has been demolished. On the left was St James' School.

Walmer Castle, 1906. Another of Kent's famous castles, this one was built as a fortress by Henry VIII but has since become a stately home. It is the official residence of the Lord Warden of the Cinque Ports, the present Warden being HM the Queen Mother. The Duke of Wellington died here in 1852.

Walmer Promenade, 1906. In the middle distance can be seen the Walmer Lifeboat House.

Charabanc on Deal seafront, summer 1921. The passengers seem to be prepared for a chilly trip to Margate.

Deal bandstand, 1906. Band concerts were very popular with Edwardian audiences and the road was closed during performances to accommodate the chairs.

Deal pier, 1924. This was the second pier to be built at Deal. It was constructed in 1864 and built of iron. The posters are advertising entertainment at the pier pavilion.

Deal from the end of the pier, 1891. Deal today has the only pleasure pier still surviving intact in Kent. It is Deal's third pier and was opened in 1957.

Deal lugger *Early Morn*. Deal luggers were renowned for rescue work along the coast. This vessel with her crew had just rescued twenty-four sailors and passengers from the SS *Strathclyde* in an accident off Dover on 17 February 1876.

Unloading a catch on Deal beach, 1952. Sea fishing was still a flourishing business at Deal in the 1950s.

High Street, Deal, 1906. The library on the corner of Park Street was run by Mudie's, the biggest chain of lending libraries in the country at this date.

High Street, Deal, 1962. This photograph of the High Street, taken nearly sixty years later, shows the same buildings but from the opposite direction. The library has now become Lipton's.

The Timeball, Deal. This tower was originally part of a signal system, to pass messages to the Admiralty during the Napoleonic Wars. It was abandoned in 1814 but in 1855 a timeball was added to the roof so that ships in The Downs could check the time against Greenwich. It is now a working museum.

Taking the salute, Deal, 1925. The Royal Marines Depot at Walmer housed all the Marine recruits until 1977. The School of Music, the final link with the Royal Marines, left Deal in 1996.

Section Five

By the Kentish Stour

Sandwich, Canterbury, Ashford

An almost Flemish-looking scene of the River Stour near The Weavers, Canterbury, probably late 1950s.

River Stour, Sandwich, 1924. Sandwich in the 1920s had a flourishing trade in timber and animal feed.

The Barbican, Sandwich, 1891. Sandwich, the fourth Cinque Port, located in Kent, is like New Romney now isolated from the sea. The fifth port was Hastings in Sussex. The bridge in the foreground of this view was subject to a toll until the 1970s.

Cattle market, Sandwich, *c.* 1900. The weekly livestock market brought a touch of excitement to the peaceful town.

Red Cow Inn, Sandwich, *c.* 1890. This hostelry, close to the cattle market, was popular with local farmers.

Strand Street, Sandwich, *c.* 1900. This was a very busy street at this time.

Strand Street, 1950s. Many of the same buildings are in both this picture and the one above. The Weavers Shop is on the corner of Three Kings Yard and weaving was still done here by hand at this time.

Canterbury Cathedral, 1886. This view of the north side of the cathedral includes the library, which was built in 1868.

Canterbury Cathedral cloisters, 1886. The chapter house is in the centre, with the Victorian library to the left. The library was bombed in 1942 but fortunately its valuable contents had previously been removed. There are no tombstones in the cloister grass today.

St Dunstan's Street and the Westgate Towers, Canterbury, 1890. This photograph shows a view still familiar today, except for the absence of traffic. The Falstaff Hotel on the left was probably a welcome sight in the days when the city gates were closed at night, when travellers arriving after curfew could stay here.

Canterbury from the Westgate, 1930s. This photograph was probably taken during Cricket Week when the main streets were decorated with flags. The 1933 Friars (Odeon) Cinema is seen, as is the tower of All Saints' Church, demolished in 1938.

Riding Gate, Canterbury, *c.* 1870. When the Romans built a wall around Canterbury (*Durovernum*) the road from Dover entered the city through a gate here. The arch in the photograph was demolished in 1883 and its replacement in turn was replaced by the present bridge in 1970.

View from the city wall near Riding Gate, Canterbury, 1952. The Riding Gate Inn on the left was damaged during the Second World War and demolished in 1955. The *Invicta* locomotive used on the Canterbury and Whitstable Railway in the 1830s was given to the city in 1906. Today it is in the Heritage Museum in Stour Street.

High Street and The Parade, Canterbury, 1921. The entrance to Mercery Lane is on the right, flanked by part of the medieval Chequer Inn building and what is now Boots the Chemist. In the twelfth century Solomon the Mercer lived on the site, and this has resulted in the street name Mercery Lane.

George and Dragon Inn, High Street, Canterbury. This old inn was demolished in 1898 and the Royal Museum and Public Library (Beaney Institute) was built on the site.

House and shop, Burgate Street, Canterbury, 1880s. No. 50 Burgate Street housed a cooper's shop before the First World War. In 1942 this part of Canterbury suffered greatly from bombing.

The Longmarket, Canterbury, early 1950s. The temporary shops were erected after wartime bombing. The postbox remains in the wall of the Corn Exchange, which was bombed. This area of Canterbury has since been rebuilt twice.

Bank Street, Ashford. The vehicle in the middle of the road is piled high with furniture. The buildings in the street have remained relatively unaltered up to the present day.

W. Richardson, Fishmonger and Poulterer, 4 Bank Street, Ashford, *c.* 1910. Mr Richardson was prominent in local government in Ashford. He is seen here in his car with his son, W.A. Richardson, standing alongside.

W. Richardson's greengrocer's shop at 9 Bank Street. This was Mr Richardson's second shop in Ashford, and later he opened a fruit and flower shop on the corner of Bank Street and Tufton Street.

Ashford Trades Exhibition, Corn Exchange, 27–29 May 1909. This was organised by a committee under the chairmanship of W. Richardson. Chas Clementson and Son, pictured here, were drapers at 108–10 High Street.

High Street, Ashford, 1910. Seen behind the horse and cart is 93 High Street, occupied by the outfitters and tailors department of Lewis and Hyland. This firm grew to become one of Ashford's largest and best known shops, trading until 1980.

A vehicle belonging to Lee and Son of Ashford. The driver is Mr Capeling and the photograph was taken in Wellesley Road where the firm had auction rooms. This long-established family business, founded in 1868, was also concerned with removals, warehousing and house furnishings.

J. Wood and Son, Ashford, *c.* 1895. Founded in 1863, the company flourished and was responsible for some of the large buildings in Ashford, such as Whitfield Hall in Bank Street. They had premises in Norwood Street and also an undertaker's business at 21 Tufton Street. On the far left is Mr E.K. Chittenden, who was apprenticed to Mr Wood but later founded his own building business with his yard in Magazine Road.

Ashford market, Elwick Street, 1989. The Tuesday stock market is shown here. Ashford has held a regular market since the thirteenth century. Originally held in the Lower High Street, the market moved to the Elwick Road site in 1856 and is now one of the largest markets in the country.

Auctioneer and staff, Ashford market, 1989. The market is well known for sheep sales, particularly for sheep from Romney Marsh.

Ashford station, 1891. The town has a long association with the railway. The station was opened on 1 December 1842.

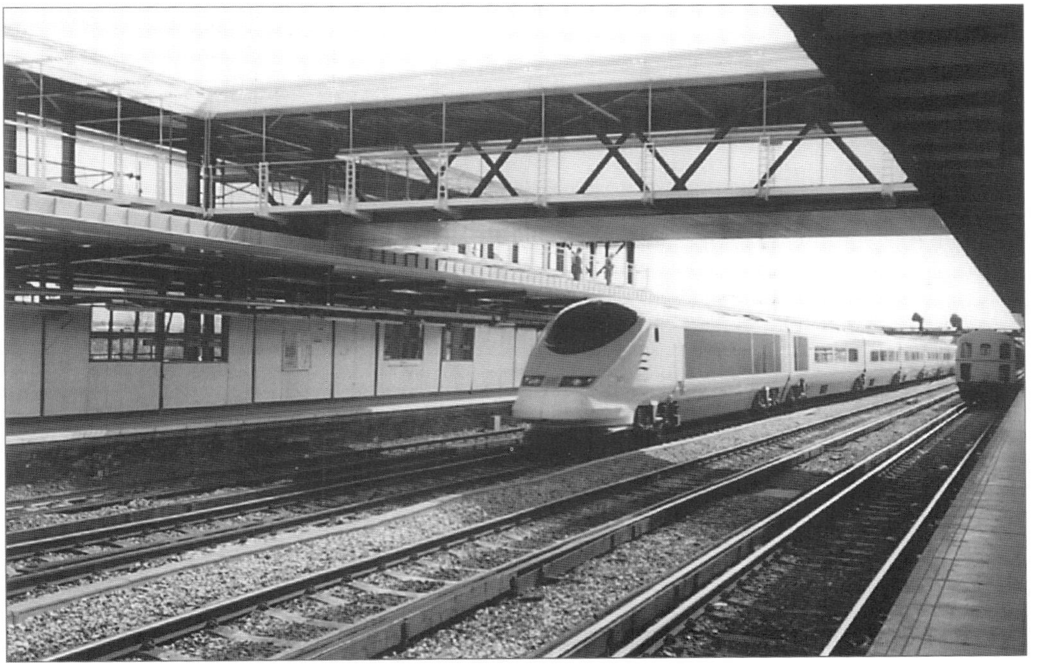

A Eurostar train passing through Ashford station, 1995. The photograph shows rebuilding work in progress on the station to transform it into Ashford International. The first Eurostar train stopped here on 8 January 1996, marking a new era for Ashford.

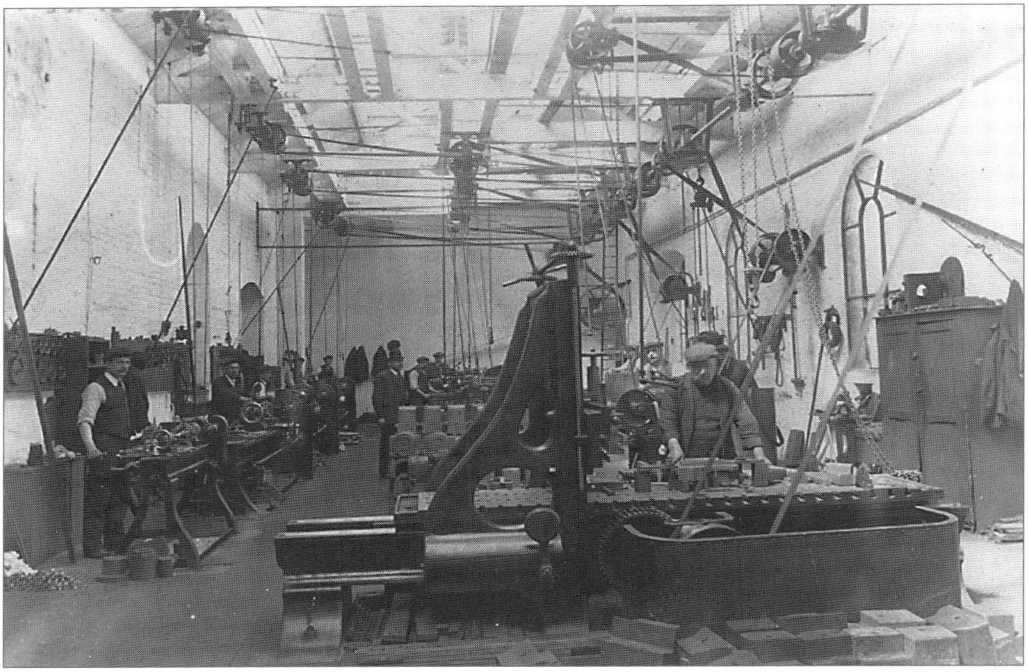

Ashford railway works, *c.* 1907. Originally founded in 1847, it gradually grew into a major centre for engineering support, at its peak in the early years of the twentieth century.

Ashford Tennis Club, *c.* 1900. The photograph shows some of Ashford's leading professional and trade families including Leslie Creery, a solicitor (back row in white), Jessie Burnage from the music shop (third row, far left) and Alice Sankey (fourth from left, third row), whose family had a grocer's shop in the High Street.

SECTION SIX

AROUND THE SWALE

Faversham, Sittingbourne & Milton, Queenborough, Sheerness

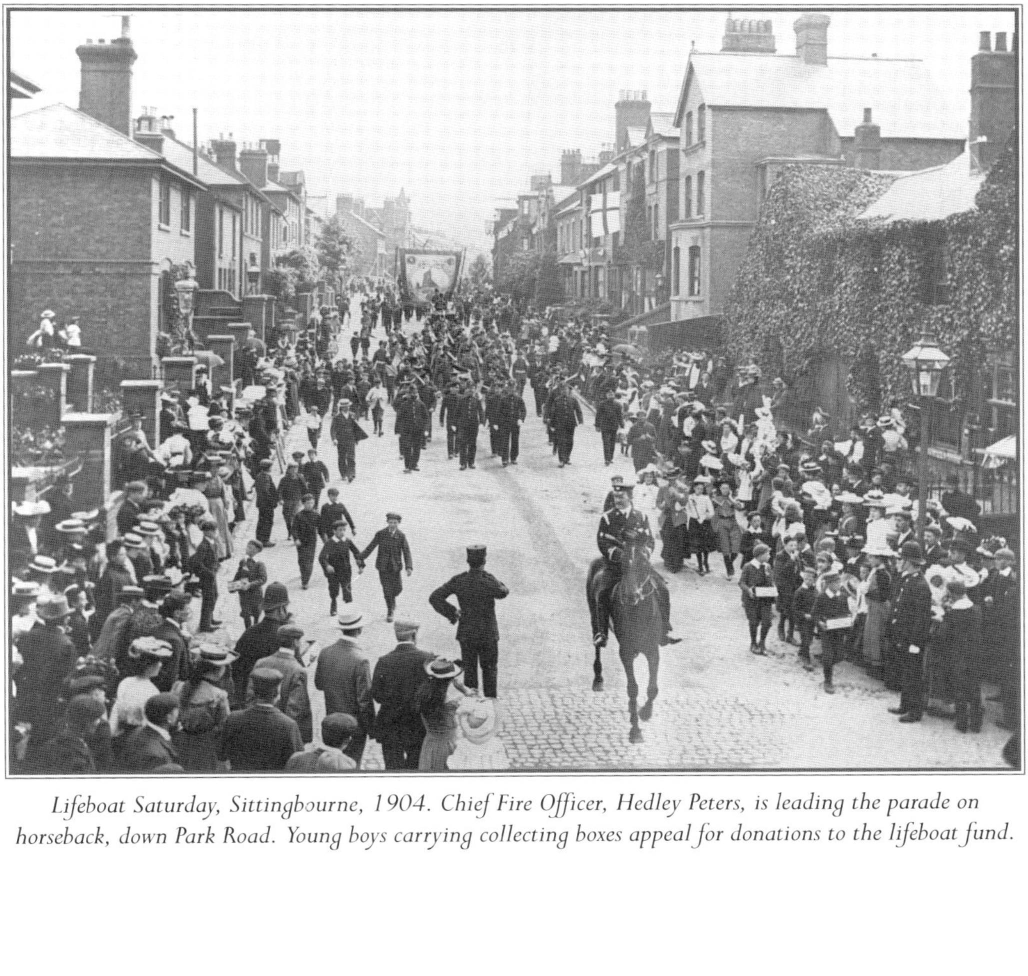

Lifeboat Saturday, Sittingbourne, 1904. Chief Fire Officer, Hedley Peters, is leading the parade on horseback, down Park Road. Young boys carrying collecting boxes appeal for donations to the lifeboat fund.

The Mall, Faversham, *c.* 1910. The drinking fountain, with a water trough for cattle and horses and a lower trough for sheep and dogs, was provided with money raised by public subscription. It came into use on 30 June 1899 and provided much-needed water for travellers on the Canterbury to London road.

The Market Place, Faversham, 1950s: a familiar view of the Market Place and Guildhall on market day. The photograph was taken before the area was pedestrianised.

East Street, Faversham, 1887. This view is unrecognisable today as the attractive buildings in the foreground were the victims of bomb damage in 1940. The imposing building in the background is the Faversham Institute, opened in 1862, which was the focus for cultural and social activity in Faversham until its demolition in 1979.

Ospringe Road, Faversham, 1890s. The Faversham Arms still exists as a pub, although the local brewery of Rigdens was bought by Whitbread and eventually closed in 1990. In the background is the heavily wooded site of the gunpowder mills, where St Anne's Park Estate now stands.

Court Street, Faversham, *c.* 1930. Prominent in the line of small shops is the large building owned by Child and Ellis Ltd, 'Drapers, Milliners, Costumiers, Outfitters etc.', who occupied the site from 1864 to 1971.

General Election day, Faversham, 19 January 1906. Workers from the Shepherd Neame Brewery are being transported to the polling station in wagons, pulled by a traction engine. The brewery's Court Street offices form the background to the scene.

Hospital donkey, Mount VAD Hospital, Faversham, 1915. The donkey seems to have been put to good use by the soldiers recovering at the hospital, as it was also photographed pulling a cart and a bath chair. The soldier standing is Sgt. Amos.

Peace Day celebrations, Faversham, 19 July 1919. The Floral Pageant is proceeding down Preston Street, and under an elegant domed canopy sits the Angel of Peace, represented by Miss Phyllis Rudgard.

Faversham Creek, *c.* 1900. This is a much painted and photographed scene easily recognisable today. The sailing barges are unloading at the timber yard and cement factory and the steam tug is the *Pioneer*, purchased by the town in 1884.

Faversham Creek and The Brents, *c.* 1910. This view looks towards the head of the creek. The Brents Church, built in 1881, and Brents Tavern are visible, as are some of the terraces of houses built for brickfield and other workers.

King's Mill Dam, Milton, *c.* 1910. St Paul's Church can be seen on the left.

Floods at Milton, 1926. This view at the corner of King Street shows a scene familiar to many residents in the past. Today the water levels are much lower, partly because of the heavy demands made by the local paper mills.

Lloyds Paper Mill, Sittingbourne, early 1900s. The paper industry has been a major source of employment in Sittingbourne for many years.

Key Street, Sittingbourne, 1920s. This scene of tranquillity is in direct contrast to today's very busy road junction. The Key Inn on the left was demolished to make room for a roundabout in the 1970s. The motorbike and sidecar in the picture belonged to the photographer.

High Street, Sittingbourne, *c.* 1910. This picture clearly shows two of Sittingbourne's old coaching inns, the Rose and the Bull. Woolworth's now occupies the site of the Rose, but the Bull Hotel, which originated in the fourteenth century, is still open for business.

High Street, Sittingbourne, 1960s. This is the junction of the High Street with Central Avenue. The former Town Hall, on the right, was demolished in 1969.

Soldiers travelling westward along Sittingbourne High Street, past the junction with Crescent Street, during the First World War.

High Street, Sittingbourne, 1960s. This is the area of the High Street shown above but the entrance to Crescent Street is on the right. The Forum Shopping Centre occupies the site at Crescent Street today.

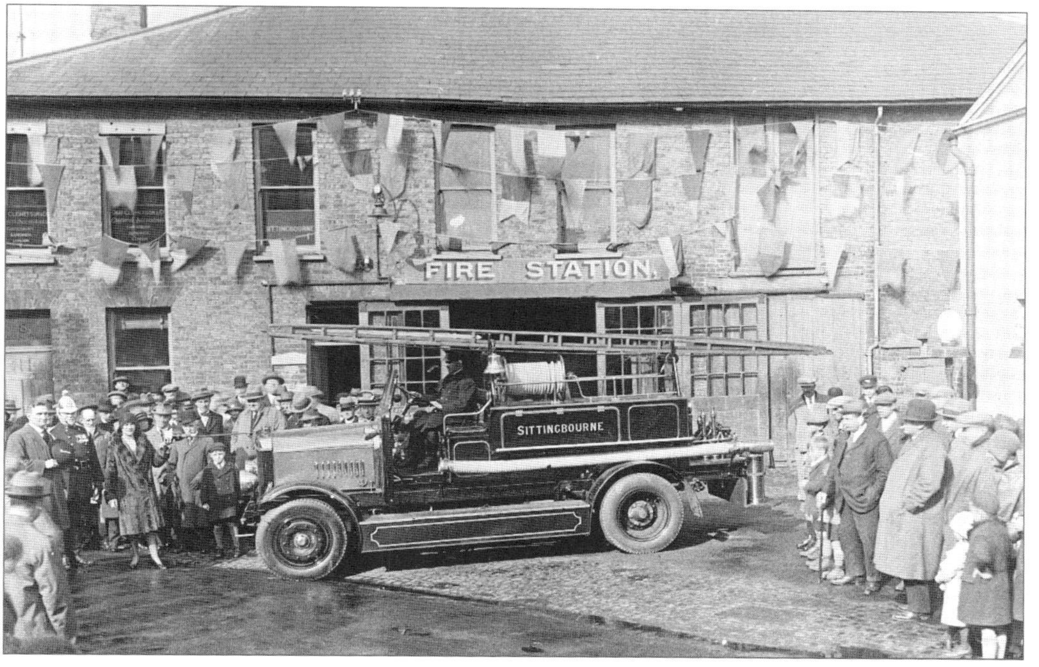

Fire station, Crescent Street, Sittingbourne, 1930. The station was decorated to celebrate the arrival of this new motorised fire engine.

The Creek, Sittingbourne, *c.* 1905. The sailing barges were vital to the cement and brick industries at the time. In the background Burley's barge yard and sail loft can be seen. They now form the Dolphin Yard Sailing Barge Museum.

High Street, Queenborough, 1829. The Guildhall with its distinctive clock is seen at the end of the row of buildings on the right. Once a 'rotten borough' Queenborough, on the Isle of Sheppey, is considered to be the last planned medieval town in England.

Guildhall, Queenborough, 1920s. The Guildhall has been well preserved and contains a good collection of regalia and other items related to the history of the town. Lord Nelson and Lady Hamilton are reputed to have lived in a house near the Guildhall.

Sheerness harbour, *c.* 1840. This detailed engraving shows a variety of naval, commercial and pleasure shipping with the dockyard buildings and the pier behind.

The Fort, Sheerness, 1860s. There has been a fort at Sheerness since the reign of Henry VIII, when he ordered one to be erected to protect the entrance to the Medway. The Garrison Point Fort pictured here was constructed in 1860.

Gunnery School, Sheerness Dockyard, *c.* 1900. The gunnery school was established in 1893 to instruct men based at Sheerness and Chatham naval barracks. Later the building was used as the shore training establishment known as HMS *Wildfire*.

Marine Parade beach, Sheerness, 1930. The opening of the Sittingbourne to Sheerness railway line in 1860 brought day trippers by the hundreds to Sheerness. The square building in the centre top of the picture is the Victoria Hotel (now Richmond House), known locally as the 'glasshouse' because of its many windows.

Bandstand and recreation ground, Sheerness, *c.* 1910. A military band is giving a performance to entertain the holiday-makers and local residents.

The Aquarena Swimming Pool, Sheerness, 1950s. This was opened in 1939 and had swimming clubs for both sexes; it was also the venue for water polo matches.

High Street, Sheerness, *c.* 1905. This view shows the tramway system which conveniently linked the main line railway from Sittingbourne to the light railway running across the Isle of Sheppey.

High Street, Sheerness, *c.* 1903. The children are posing for the photographer in this view, which shows a roof line that has hardly changed today.

SECTION SEVEN

DOWN BY THE SEASIDE

Whitstable, Herne Bay, Margate, Broadstairs, Ramsgate

Empire Bandstand and open-air dance floor, East Cliff, Ramsgate, 1950s.

Whitstable harbour, probably mid-1950s, when pleasure boats shared the harbour with working vessels. The harbour dates from 1832 and until 1958 was owned by successive railway operators.

Harbour Street, Whitstable, *c.* 1910. The castellated building known as Harbour Buildings was constructed in 1905.

Marine Terrace, Whitstable, *c.* 1950. The public house on the left is the Old Neptune which replaced an earlier pub on the site, destroyed in a flood in 1897. The Old Neptune was itself damaged in the severe floods of 1953.

West Beach, Whitstable, *c.* 1910. The tents are in front of the row of houses known as Wave Crest.

High Street, Whitstable, *c.* 1900. The street seems to be full of public houses with the Duke of Cumberland Hotel in the centre, the sign of the Bear and Key on the right and The Royal Naval Reserve on the left.

High Street, Whitstable, 1920s. This view is showing more of the street than the previous picture, but is taken looking in the same direction. In the centre is the boot warehouse of Freeman, Hardy and Willis. Today Whitstable still retains many of its small shops.

Tankerton, 1890. This view was taken in the year that the Tankerton Estate Company Ltd was established to develop the area as a resort.

The beach, Tankerton, *c.* 1910. In the background are some of the tea booths which were popular with visitors. An Edwardian guidebook writer said that Tankerton was 'one of the few quiet places where families and children can still enjoy themselves unhampered by the often expensive customs of more fashionable resorts'.

Shopping centre, Sea View Holiday Camp, Swalecliffe, 1950s. A camp of caravans and chalets still exists.

Horse-drawn omnibus, Herne Bay, *c*. 1900. This served the station, hotels and East Cliff.

Ship Inn, Herne Bay, 1890. The inn is much older than Herne Bay. It marks the end of the old road from Canterbury, and the resort began to develop around it in the late eighteenth and early nineteenth centuries. There was a fight near the inn in 1821 when a smuggler killed Midshipman Snow of the Coast Blockade.

West Cliff Beach, Herne Bay, 1950s. The traditional beach huts were very popular as was the pier, the second longest in England.

Herne Bay pier. This was Herne Bay's third pier, built from 1896 to 1899 as an extension of the second pier, made longer so that steamboats could land and take on passengers. The rails laid down for the crane during the building work were left and used by a tram. Sadly the pier was badly damaged by a storm in 1978 and most of it has gone.

Herne Bay pier, 1927. The pier theatre at the entrance was built in 1884 and burnt down in 1928. The pavilion built in 1910 could seat over 2,000 people and met the same fate in 1970.

Marine Parade East, Herne Bay, 1896. In the background can be seen the clock tower and the pier.

Marine Parade and Tower Gardens, 1927. The clock tower is a local landmark and was given to the town by Mrs Ann Thwaytes in 1837.

Herne Bay bandstand, 1927. The bandstand was opened in 1924 and in 1932 a roofed screen was built around the enclosure, leaving only the centre open.

Children's Corner, Herne Bay, *c.* 1950. The entertainer is probably Uncle Colin.

Marine Sands, Margate, *c.* 1900. The minstrels are performing on the sands. Margate as a resort dates from 1736 when the first sea water baths were advertised. Judging by the number of bathing machines in this view, there was no lack of sea bathers in 1900.

Royal Sea Bathing Hospital, Margate, *c.* 1890. It opened in 1796 as 'a place where poor patients could take the sea water cure in the battle against consumption'. Opened with just twenty-five patients, by 1830 it was treating 541.

Margate Harbour, *c.* 1900. The harbour is sheltered by the stone pier and in the centre of the view is the Droit House, where tolls and harbour dues were collected by the Margate Pier and Harbour Company.

Storm damage, Margate harbour, 1877. During a great storm the hull of a sailing vessel that had been wrecked on rocks three weeks before broke up, one portion cutting through the jetty. The distant vessels are stranded on the rocks.

The jetty, Margate, *c*. 1910. In other towns this structure would be known as the pier, but at Margate it was always called the jetty and the jetty was known as the stone pier. The paddle steamer approaching is the *Golden Eagle*. The jetty was virtually destroyed in a storm in 1978.

Fort bandstand, Margate, *c*. 1910. There were daily performances during the summer. In 1911 this bandstand was moved to Queen's Promenade, and the Winter Gardens constructed here in an artificial hollow.

Dane Park, Margate. The park was opened in 1897 by the Lord Mayor of London. It originally included a bandstand, lakes and rockeries, summer house, tennis courts and an outer grass cycle and trotting track.

Cecil Square, Margate, 12 May 1937. The crowds are celebrating the coronation of George VI. Bobby's was a popular department store; Marks and Spencer is now on the same site.

The Parade, Margate, *c.* 1910. From 1901 to 1937 trams ran between Margate, Broadstairs and Ramsgate. The Metropole Hotel, in the centre of the picture, was the scene of a famous murder in 1929, when Sidney Fox murdered his mother there.

Marine Sands, Margate, 1935. This area was in its heyday at this time with the Marine Bathing Pavilion completed in 1926 and the Dreamland Cinema opening in 1935 with seating for 2,200 people.

Lido Bathing Pool, Margate, late 1940s. This took two years to build and opened in 1927. It was a sea water pool and was surrounded by an entertainments complex of cafés, concert hall, bars, bandstand and hot sea- and fresh-water baths.

Newgate Gap, Margate, 1908. A scene showing Edwardian holiday-makers with the new stone bridge at Newgate Gap, which had been built in 1907 to celebrate fifty years since Margate's incorporation as a borough. The Highcliffe Hotel is seen on the left.

Hodges Gap, Margate, 1908. Bridges were built over the gaps previously only used by farmers collecting seaweed. This iron bridge was replaced by a new bridge in 1912 and again in 1993. The donkeys in the foreground are very appropriate to this scene, as Margate was the first seaside resort to popularise donkey rides.

Queen's Promenade from Hodges Bridge, 1935. The very popular Bungalow Tea Gardens is on the left, and lining the Eastern Esplanade are large hotels.

High Street, St Peter's, Broadstairs, 1896. The Crown and Thistle Public House is on the left. The Ramsgate brewer Tomson and Wotton was England's oldest brewery, having been in business since 1554.

Dickens Festival, Broadstairs. This annual festival, held in June, is a reminder of the many times Charles Dickens stayed in the town between 1837 and 1851. A number of his books were partially written here, including *David Copperfield, The Old Curiosity Shop* and *The Pickwick Papers*.

Main Bay, now called Viking Bay, Broadstairs, 1907. Bathing machines are much in evidence and a Thames barge is unloading on the right of the picture.

Arrival of the Viking ship *Hugin*, Main Bay, Broadstairs, 28 July 1949. This replica ship was rowed from Denmark by young men of Copenhagen, to commemorate the 1,500th anniversary of the reputed first landing in Kent of Vikings led by Hengist and Horsa. Main Bay was afterwards called Viking Bay and the ship is now on display at Pegwell Bay, Ramsgate.

Broadstairs harbour, 1912. Wherries can be seen in the foreground, the building in the centre of Harbour Street is The Tartar Frigate public house and above it on the skyline is Bleak House, formerly known as Fort House. On the extreme right is the pier lookout and boatmen's store.

Pier lookout and boatmen's store, Broadstairs harbour, 1950: a close-up view of the building visible in the previous picture. Above the door is a ship's figurehead, from a Spanish brig that came ashore in 1844, and surrounding it are rib bones of a 70-ton whale washed up in February 1762.

George Strevens mending nets, Broadstairs harbour, 1979.

Edward Heath enjoying a drink at The Tartar Frigate, Broadstairs harbour. The Rt Hon. Sir Edward Heath was born in Broadstairs and attended Chatham House School, Ramsgate. He was a member of Broadstairs Sailing Club and conducted the annual Christmas Carol Concert in his home town for many years.

Uncle Mack and children, Broadstairs, 1929. James Henry Summerson (Uncle Mack) first came to Broadstairs in 1895 and entertained children and visitors with his minstrel troupe. He died in 1949 and a commemorative plaque to him, paid for by public subscription, is on the Promenade.

Victoria Home and Hospital, Broadstairs, *c.* 1895. This was one of many seaside branches of London children's homes and was opened by Princess Louise, a daughter of Queen Victoria, on 21 June 1892.

The Harbour, Ramsgate, mid-1930s. In the centre of this busy scene is the Tidal Ball.

Ramsgate Sands, 'Merrie England' and harbour, Ramsgate, 1937. This picture shows the resort at the height of its popularity.

Ramsgate Sands, 1907. An earlier view looking in the opposite direction from the previous picture. Ramsgate Sands railway station, which closed in 1926, is on the left. It also shows the Promenade Pier, completed in 1881 and demolished in 1930.

Ramsgate Sands, 1933: a similar viewpoint from the previous picture, but the 'Merrie England' amusements complex is now built. The tea stand in the foreground was famous for its teapot tea and its slogan 'No urns used here'.

Sands Concert Party, Ramsgate, 1930s. The performers are Harry Gold's Yachtsmen. Harry Gold was, in fact, Patrick Henry James Ricks, an Irishman who started performing in Ramsgate in 1897 and whose last season was in 1939. He died in 1946 aged seventy-nine.

Pegwell Road, Pegwell Bay, Ramsgate, 1907. The Bellevue Tavern on the right was famous for its shrimp teas and opposite was Bangers, where shrimp paste was made and sold in china pots with local views on the lids.

Ramsgate Historical Pageant, 1934. The pageant was performed by local people to celebrate fifty years since the incorporation of Ramsgate as a borough. They are enacting the coming of St Augustine to Kent in AD 597. He is believed to have landed at nearby Ebbsfleet.

Bull and George Hotel, High Street, Ramsgate, after a Zeppelin raid, 17 May 1915. After the First World War the site was acquired by Woolworth's, which opened in 1920.

Officers with bombs, outside the old police station, Charlotte Court, Ramsgate, May 1915. These were the bombs dropped in the Zeppelin raid. Ramsgate was the most heavily bombed town in England during the First World War.

Football match on the Goodwin Sands, 21 July 1952. The Goodwin Sands, off the Kent coast, have been through the centuries a notoriously dangerous area for shipping. Ramsgate boatmen and the later lifeboats were kept busy with the shipwrecks.

ACKNOWLEDGEMENTS

I wish to thank the following for permission to reproduce photographs contained in this book. (The numbers are page numbers, and t and b refer to a picture's position on the page, top or bottom.) Tonbridge Historical Society: 4, 55–8, 113 (t); G. Porter: 9 (b), 18 (b); Gordon Anckorn: 20 (t), 22–8; The Malling Society: 29 (b), 30, back cover; George Burningham-Cate: 37 (t); Rochester upon Medway City Archives: 43 (t); H.S. Cousins: 105 (b); Andrew Brown: 113 (b); Mrs H. Jones: 114 (t); Tony Bryan: 151 (t); Francis Frith Collection (purchased with rights to reproduce): 32, 49 (b), 50 (b), 51 (b), 53 (b), 54, 60 (b), 61 (b), 66 (b), 68 (b), 99, 102 (b), 107 (b), 116 (b), 123 (b), 124 (b), 129 (b), 132 (t), 133 (t), 136 (t), 137 (b), 140 (b).

Every effort has been made to trace the known copyright owners. Some photographs, however, which have been in library collections for many years do not have details about the copyright owner. Should this information subsequently become available we will make acknowledgement in any future editions of this work.

The illustrations are from the collections found in the following libraries and studies centres: Ashford Library: 108–12, 113 (b), 114; Broadstairs Library: 148 (t), 149 (b), 150 (b), 151, 152 (t); Canterbury Library: 99, 103 (b), 104 (b), 105, 106 (b), 107; Chatham Library: 37 (b); Dartford Library: 7–12, 158; Deal Library: 94 (t), 96 (b), 98 (b); Dover Library: 88–9, 90 (b), 91–2; Faversham Library: 116–20; Folkestone Library: 73 (b), 76 (b), 82 (t), 83, 84 (b), 86 (t), 87 (b); Gillingham Library: 33–5; Gravesend Library: 13 (b), 14, 15 (b), 16–17; Herne Bay Library: 138 (t); Hythe Library: 81 (t); Maidstone Library: 49 (t); Margate Library: 141–5, 146 (t), 147 (b); Ramsgate Library: 131, 153–4, 155 (t), 156–7; Rochester upon Medway Studies Centre: title page, 31, 36 (b), 37 (t), 38, 40–6; Sevenoaks Library (Gordon Anckorn Collection): 20 (t), 22–8; Sheerness Library: 127 (b), 129; Sittingbourne Library: 115, 121–2, 123 (b), 124; Swanley Library: 18 (t), 19; Tenterden Library: 59, 69–71; Tonbridge Library (Tonbridge Historical Society Collection): 4, 55–8, 113 (t); Tunbridge Wells Library: 62 (t), 63, 64 (t), 65 (b), 66 (t); Whitstable Library: 132 (t), 133 (t), 136 (t); Centre for Kentish Studies (Gerald Edgeler Collection): 2, 29 (t), 47–8; (Freda Barton Collection – The Malling Society): back cover, 29 (b), 30. All other illustrations which are not listed above are from the collection at the Centre for Kentish Studies.

The inauguration of the Dartford Tramway Service, 1906.

BRITAIN IN OLD PHOTOGRAPHS

berystwyth & North Ceredigion
round Abingdon
cton
lderney: A Second Selection
long the Avon from Stratford to Tewkesbury
ltrincham
mersham
round Amesbury
nglesey
rnold & Bestwood
rnold & Bestwood: A Second Selection
rundel & the Arun Valley
shbourne
round Ashby-de-la-Zouch
vro Aircraft
ylesbury
alham & Tooting
anburyshire
arnes, Mortlake & Sheen
arnsley
ath
eaconsfield
edford
edfordshire at Work
edworth
everley
exley
ideford
ilston
rmingham Railways
ishop's Stortford & Sawbridgeworth
shopstone & Seaford
shopstone & Seaford: A Second Selection
ack Country Aviation
ack Country Railways
ack Country Road Transport
ackburn
lackpool
round Blandford Forum
letchley
olton
ournemouth
radford
raintree & Bocking at Work
recon
rentwood
ridgwater & the River Parrett
ridlington
ridport & the Bride Valley
rierley Hill
righton & Hove
righton & Hove: A Second Selection
ristol
round Bristol
rixton & Norwood
arly Broadstairs & St Peters
romley, Keston & Hayes

Buckingham & District
Burford
Bury
Bushbury
Camberwell
Cambridge
Cannock Yesterday & Today
Canterbury: A Second Selection
Castle Combe to Malmesbury
Chadwell Heath
Chard & Ilminster
Chatham Dockyard
Chatham & Gillingham
Cheadle
Cheam & Belmont
Chelmsford
Cheltenham: A Second Selection
Cheltenham at War
Cheltenham in the 1950s
Chepstow & the River Wye
Chesham Yesterday & Today
Cheshire Railways
Chester
Chippenham & Lacock
Chiswick
Chorley & District
Cirencester
Around Cirencester
Clacton-on-Sea
Around Clitheroe
Clwyd Railways
Clydesdale
Colchester
Colchester 1940–70
Colyton & Seaton
The Cornish Coast
Corsham & Box
The North Cotswolds
Coventry: A Second Selection
Around Coventry
Cowes & East Cowes
Crawley New Town
Around Crawley
Crewkerne & the Ham Stone Villages
Cromer
Croydon
Crystal Palace, Penge & Anerley
Darlington
Darlington: A Second Selection
Dawlish & Teignmouth
Deal
Derby
Around Devizes
Devon Aerodromes
East Devon at War
Around Didcot & the Hagbournes
Dorchester
Douglas
Dumfries
Dundee at Work
Durham People

Durham at Work
Ealing & Northfields
East Grinstead
East Ham
Eastbourne
Elgin
Eltham
Ely
Enfield
Around Epsom
Esher
Evesham to Bredon
Exeter
Exmouth & Budleigh Salterton
Fairey Aircraft
Falmouth
Farnborough
Farnham: A Second Selection
Fleetwood
Folkestone: A Second Selection
Folkestone: A Third Selection
The Forest of Dean
Frome
Fulham
Galashiels
Garsington
Around Garstang
Around Gillingham
Gloucester
Gloucester: from the Walwin Collection
North Gloucestershire at War
South Gloucestershire at War
Gosport
Goudhurst to Tenterden
Grantham
Gravesend
Around Gravesham
Around Grays
Great Yarmouth
Great Yarmouth: A Second Selection
Greenwich & Woolwich
Grimsby
Around Grimsby
Grimsby Docks
Gwynedd Railways
Hackney: A Second Selection
Hackney: A Third Selection
From Haldon to Mid-Dartmoor
Hammersmith & Shepherds Bush
Hampstead to Primrose Hill
Harrow & Pinner
Hastings
Hastings: A Second Selection
Haverfordwest
Hayes & West Drayton
Around Haywards Heath
Around Heathfield
Around Heathfield: A Second Selection
Around Helston

Around Henley-on-Thames
Herefordshire
Herne Bay
Heywood
The High Weald
The High Weald: A Second Selection
Around Highworth
Around Highworth & Faringdon
Hitchin
Holderness
Honiton & the Otter Valley
Horsham & District
Houghton-le-Spring & Hetton-le-Hole
Houghton-le-Spring & Hetton-le-Hole: A Second Selection
Huddersfield: A Second Selection
Huddersfield: A Third Selection
Ilford
Ilfracombe
Ipswich: A Second Selection
Islington
Jersey: A Third Selection
Kendal
Kensington & Chelsea
East Kent at War
Keswick & the Central Lakes
Around Keynsham & Saltford
The Changing Face of Keynsham
Kingsbridge
Kingston
Kinver
Kirkby & District
Kirkby Lonsdale
Around Kirkham
Knowle & Dorridge
The Lake Counties at Work
Lancashire
The Lancashire Coast
Lancashire North of the Sands
Lancashire Railways
East Lancashire at War
Around Lancaster
Lancing & Sompting
Around Leamington Spa
Around Leamington Spa: A Second Selection
Leeds in the News
Leeds Road & Rail
Around Leek
Leicester
The Changing Face of Leicester
Leicester at Work
Leicestershire People
Around Leighton Buzzard & Linslade
Letchworth
Lewes
Lewisham & Deptford: A Second Selection
Lichfield

Lincoln
Lincoln Cathedral
The Lincolnshire Coast
Liverpool
Around Llandudno
Around Lochaber
Theatrical London
Around Louth
The Lower Fal Estuary
Lowestoft
Luton
Lympne Airfield
Lytham St Annes
Maidenhead
Around Maidenhead
Around Malvern
Manchester
Manchester Road & Rail
Mansfield
Marlborough: A Second Selection
Marylebone & Paddington
Around Matlock
Melton Mowbray
Around Melksham
The Mendips
Merton & Morden
Middlesbrough
Midsomer Norton & Radstock
Around Mildenhall
Milton Keynes
Minehead
Monmouth & the River Wye
The Nadder Valley
Newark
Around Newark
Newbury
Newport, Isle of Wight
The Norfolk Broads
Norfolk at War
North Fylde
North Lambeth
North Walsham & District
Northallerton
Northampton
Around Norwich
Nottingham 1944–74
The Changing Face of Nottingham
Victorian Nottingham
Nottingham Yesterday & Today
Nuneaton
Around Oakham
Ormskirk & District
Otley & District
Oxford: The University
Oxford Yesterday & Today
Oxfordshire Railways: A Second Selection
Oxfordshire at School
Around Padstow
Pattingham & Wombourne
Penwith
Penzance & Newlyn
Around Pershore
Around Plymouth
Poole
Portsmouth
Poulton-le-Fylde
Preston
Prestwich
Pudsey
Radcliffe
RAF Chivenor
RAF Cosford
RAF Hawkinge
RAF Manston
RAF Manston: A Second Selection
RAF St Mawgan
RAF Tangmere
Ramsgate & Thanet Life
Reading
Reading: A Second Selection
Redditch & the Needle District
Redditch: A Second Selection
Richmond, Surrey
Rickmansworth
Around Ripley
The River Soar
Romney Marsh
Romney Marsh: A Second Selection
Rossendale
Around Rotherham
Rugby
Around Rugeley
Ruislip
Around Ryde
St Albans
St Andrews
Salford
Salisbury
Salisbury: A Second Selection
Salisbury: A Third Selection
Around Salisbury
Sandhurst & Crowthorne
Sandown & Shanklin
Sandwich
Scarborough
Scunthorpe
Seaton, Lyme Regis & Axminster
Around Seaton & Sidmouth
Sedgley & District
The Severn Vale
Sherwood Forest
Shrewsbury
Shrewsbury: A Second Selection
Shropshire Railways
Skegness
Around Skegness
Skipton & the Dales
Around Slough
Smethwick
Somerton & Langport
Southampton
Southend-on-Sea
Southport
Southwark
Southwell
Southwold to Aldeburgh
Stafford
Around Stafford
Staffordshire Railways
Around Staveley
Stepney
Stevenage
The History of Stilton Cheese
Stoke-on-Trent
Stoke Newington
Stonehouse to Painswick
Around Stony Stratford
Around Stony Stratford: A Second Selection
Stowmarket
Streatham
Stroud & the Five Valleys
Stroud & the Five Valleys: A Second Selection
Stroud's Golden Valley
The Stroudwater and Thames & Severn Canals
The Stroudwater and Thames & Severn Canals: A Second Selection
Suffolk at Work
Suffolk at Work: A Second Selection
The Heart of Suffolk
Sunderland
Sutton
Swansea
Swindon: A Third Selection
Swindon: A Fifth Selection
Around Tamworth
Taunton
Around Taunton
Teesdale
Teesdale: A Second Selection
Tenbury Wells
Around Tettenhall & Codshall
Tewkesbury & the Vale of Gloucester
Thame to Watlington
Around Thatcham
Around Thirsk
Thornbury to Berkeley
Tipton
Around Tonbridge
Trowbridge
Around Truro
TT Races
Tunbridge Wells
Tunbridge Wells: A Second Selection
Twickenham
Uley, Dursley & Cam
The Upper Fal
The Upper Tywi Valley
Uxbridge, Hillingdon & Cowley
The Vale of Belvoir
The Vale of Conway
Ventnor
Wakefield
Wallingford
Walsall
Waltham Abbey
Wandsworth at War
Wantage, Faringdon & the Vale Villages
Around Warwick
Weardale
Weardale: A Second Selection
Wednesbury
Wells
Welshpool
West Bromwich
West Wight
Weston-super-Mare
Around Weston-super-Mare
Weymouth & Portland
Around Wheatley
Around Whetstone
Whitchurch to Market Drayton
Around Whitstable
Wigton & the Solway Plain
Willesden
Around Wilton
Wimbledon
Around Windsor
Wingham, Addisham & Littlebourne
Wisbech
Witham & District
Witney
Around Witney
The Witney District
Wokingham
Around Woodbridge
Around Woodstock
Woolwich
Woolwich Royal Arsenal
Around Wootton Bassett, Cricklade & Purton
Worcester
Worcester in a Day
Around Worcester
Worcestershire at Work
Around Worthing
Wotton-under-Edge to Chipping Sodbury
Wymondham & Attleborough
The Yorkshire Wolds